GRANNY NORB

and the Cave Troll

By: Malcolm J. Hogan

Art and Design by Nick Oldham

Published in the UK by

GRANNY NORBAG

A CIP record of this book is available from the British Library.

First printed 2019 by B&B Press (Parkgate) Ltd., Aldwarke Rd, Parkgate, Rotherham S62 6DY.

www.grannynorbag.co.uk

ISBN 978 1 9993216 1 1

Other GRANNY NORBAG titles available:
GRANNY NORBAG AND THE NAUGHTY PIRATES

Dedicated to Malcolm and Nick's wives,
for all their support, patience and understanding.

One bright Tuesday morning, Granny Norbag was having her hair styled
by Monsieur Alfonzo, her mobile hairdresser.

A disgruntled Engelbert put his wings in his ears as the noisy hair dryer was turned on.

Looking through her newspaper, Granny Norbag spotted a headline about a missing rainbow.

"I wish I could visit the end of a rainbow!" she called out to a confused Engelbert.

Seeming to hear Granny Norbag's wish the enchanted false teeth began to chatter.

She tried hard NOT to say the magic words but the teeth could not be stopped.

Suddenly the room began to spin. A shocked Granny Norbag just managed to grab Engelbert and her handbag, before she disappeared into the giant hair dryer.

Landing on a wooden bench, Granny Norbag and Engelbert found themselves in a gloomy leprechaun village.

"This isn't right Engelbert," the old lady observed. "Leprechauns are supposed to be happy."

A tearful leprechaun named Fox explained that a nasty Cave Troll had blocked off the entrance to Rainbow Village.

"Even the rainbow that brought us good fortune has vanished," he sobbed.

Seeing the leprechauns
SO sad and hungry, the kind
pensioner pulled out
a magnificent picnic from
her handbag.
Bravely she promised them
that she would deal with
the mean Cave Troll.

A short time later, cheered on by the excited leprechauns, Granny Norbag marched towards the cave entrance.

Engelbert circled her head feeling uneasy. He'd heard a lot of things about the Cave Troll and she did not sound nice at all.

From inside the dark cave, the Cave Troll saw Granny Norbag approaching.

Holding a large club in her muscly arm, she bounded out onto the path determined to scare the old woman away.

Standing over eight feet tall, with mighty muscles and flaming red hair, the Cave Troll towered over the tiny pensioner.

Hiding her fear, Granny Norbag smiled and offered the Cave Troll some tea and a slice of lemon drizzle cake.

Angrily the Cave Troll, who was clearly in no mood for cake, threw a sharp spear at Granny Norbag. The speedy pensioner jumped out of the way, narrowly avoiding the javelin. Screaming furiously, the beast hurled another and then another...

No matter how hard the troll tried to hit her, the nimble OAP managed to cartwheel, backflip and somersault out of the way.

Whilst Granny Norbag was dodging the spears, brave Engelbert flew near to the troll's head. He squawked loudly in her ear to distract her.

Admiring his colourful feathers, the huge brute decided that she wanted Engelbert....

...AND SHE ALWAYS GOT WHAT SHE WANTED!!!

"There's no need for all this fighting!" Granny Norbag pleaded. "You'll have lots of friends if you're nice."

"I do not want friends, wrinkle face!" snapped the stubborn troll.

Granny Norbag was most upset. She did not like name calling or bullies. As the Cave Troll tried to hit her with a heavy club, the old woman flung forward her powerful handbag.

Now feeling extremely annoyed, the Cave Troll snatched Engelbert from the air and threw a beehive at the old lady,

Thinking that Granny Norbag was a flower, the bees swarmed around her fluffy pink hair. Granny had no choice but to dive into a nearby pond.

[illegible]e Troll giggled
[illegible] sealed
Th[illegible]ve entrance
with a ginormous rock.

No matter how hard
Granny Norbag pushed and pulled,
the rock would not budge.

But Granny Norbag would never give up on her best friend. Calling on every bit of strength she had, she began to lift the rock with her bare hands.
Slowly it began to move. She lifted it higher and higher before throwing it to the ground.

"Nobody takes my Engelbert!" she exclaimed.

Dashing into the cave, Granny Norbag was shocked by what she saw.
Posing like a pop star, Engelbert was singing merrily as the Cave Troll painted his portrait.

The painting was **MAGNIFICENT!**

A surprised Granny Norbag looked around her and was amazed to see beautiful paintings all over the cave walls.

"Astounding!" she gasped admiringly.

Unaware the Cave Troll was running towards her, Granny Norbag declared, "These are the best paintings I've ever seen!"

The Cave Troll stopped in her tracks. Nobody had ever said anything nice about her before.

Later, as Granny gave her a makeover, the Cave Troll explained she wanted to be a famous artist but was too shy to show her work to anyone. She even told Granny Norbag her real name was Mandy Wartroll.

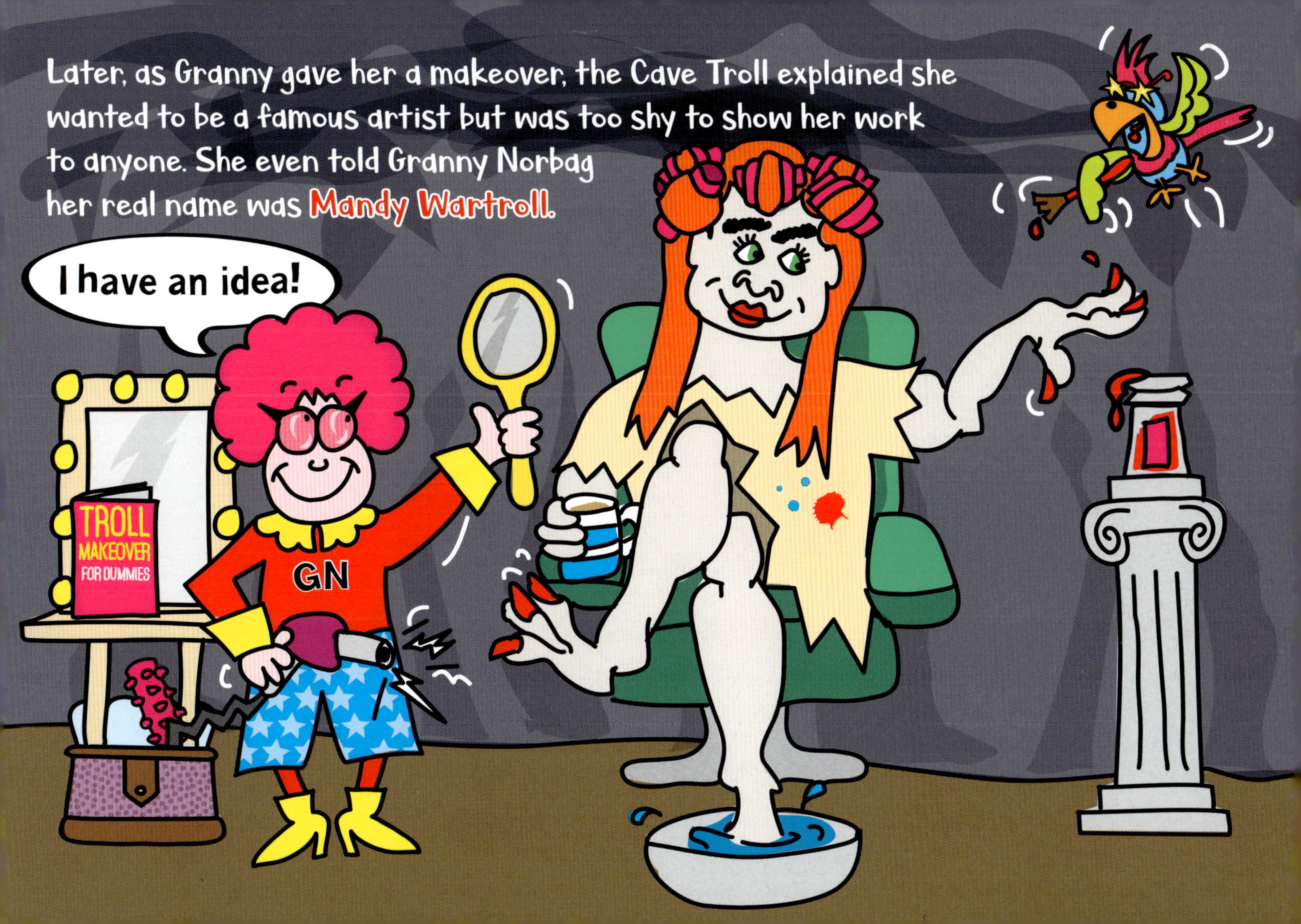

News began to spread about the amazing cave art at the end of the rainbow.

People travelled from far and wide to see Mandy's colourful paintings.

Even the King and Queen visited to present Mandy Wartroll with a special award.

"I'm very proud of you," Granny Norbag whispered to a smiling Mandy.

A happy Granny Norbag waved goodbye to her new friends as the magic teeth began to chatter once more.

Then the cave started to spin and in no time at all....

...the old woman and Engelbert were back in their living room.
'Oh no!" Monsieur Alfonzo shrieked.
"Your hair! It's ruined!"

Glancing in a mirror,
Granny Norbag saw that her hair looked just like a rainbow.
"My hair is perfect!" she laughed. "Thank you, Monsieur Alfonzo."

And this, my friends, is how our story ends.
With Granny Norbag and Engelbert hanging up paintings
that a famous artist had kindly given to them.

’Bye for now! See you in our next adventure!

In the meantime,
you can see more of what
Granny Norbag and Engelbert
are getting up to at:

@grannynorbag

@grannynorbag

@grannynorbagbooks

www.grannynorbag.co.uk

Join Granny Norbag in her next adventure
as she takes part in the Intergalactic Games...
...with some
SURPRISING
results!!!